Pray it in Latin

by

Louis G. A. Pizzuti

Syracuse, NY
2006

Pronunciation Notes

The aim in this manual has been to render the pronunciation of the Latin of the Church's prayers in such a way that it can be easily learned by a typical English speaker, and to render a word-by-word translation of the Latin so that the person praying in Latin would understand the words of their prayer.

My hope and prayer is that all those who wish to pray in the Official Language of the Church would be able to do so.

Louis Pizzuti, Sept 2, 2006

1. Latin and English Section

A.   Basic Prayers

The Sign of the Cross

In the name of the Father, and of the Son, and of the Holy Spirit.
Amen.

In nomine Patris et Filii et
Een NOH-mee-nay PAH-trees ayt FEE-lee-yee ayt
In name of-Father and of-Son and

Spiritus Sancti. Amen.
SPEE-ree-toos SAHNK-tee AH-mayn
of-Spirit of-Holy Amen

Hail Mary

Hail, Mary, full of grace, the Lord is with you. Blessed are you
among women, and blessed is the fruit of your womb, Jesus. Holy
Mary, Mother of God, pray for us sinners, now and at the hour of
our death. Amen.

Ave Maria, gratia plena, Dominus tecum,
AH-vay Maria GRAHT-see-ah PLAY-nah DOH-mee-noos TAY-koom
Hail Mary filled with-grace Lord with-you

benedicta tu in mulieribus,
bay-nay-DEEK-tah TOO een moo-lee-AY-ree-boos
blessed you among women

et benedictus fructus ventris tui, Jesus.
ayt bay-nay-DEEK-toos FROOK-toos VAYN-trees TOO-ee YAY-soos
and blessed fruit womb yours Jesus

Sancta Maria Mater Dei
SAHNK-tah Maria MAH-tayr DAY-ee
Holy Mary Mother of-God

ora pro nobis peccatoribus
OH-rah pro NOH-bees payk-ah-TOHY-ree-boos
pray for us sinners

nunc et in hora mortis nostræ. Amen.
noonk ayt een HOH-rah MOHR-tees NOHS-tray AH-mayn
Now and in hour of-death of-ours Amen

3

The Apostle's Creed

I believe in God, the Father almighty, Creator of heaven and earth. I believe in Jesus Christ, His only Son, our Lord. He was conceived by the power of the Holy Spirit and born of the Virgin Mary. He suffered under Pontius Pilate, was crucified, died, and was buried. He descended to the dead. On the third day He rose again. He ascended into heaven and sits at the right hand of God, the Father Almighty. From thence He shall come to judge the living and the dead. I believe in the Holy Spirit, the holy catholic Church, the communion of saints, the forgiveness of sins, the resurrection of the body, and the life everlasting. Amen.

Credo in Deum Patrem omnipotentem,
KRAY-doh een DAY-oom PAH-traym ohm-nee-poh-TAYN-taym
I-believe in God Father almighty

Creatorem cæli et terræ.
kray-ah-TOH-raym CHAY-lee ayt TAY-ray
Creator of-heaven and of-earth

Et in Iesum Christum,
ayt een YAY-soom KREES-toom
And in Jesus Christ

Filium eius unicum, Dominum nostrum,
FEE-lee-oom AY-yoos OO-nee-koom DOH-mee-noom NOHS-troom
Son his only, Lord ours

qui conceptus est de Spiritu Sancto,
KWEE kohn-CHAYP-toos ayst day SPEE-ree-too SAHNK-toh
who conceived was from Spirit Holy

natus ex Maria Virgine,
NAH-toos ayks Maria VEER-jee-nay
born out-of Mary Virgin

passus sub Pontio Pilato,
PAH-soos soob POHNT-see-oh pee-LAH-toh
suffered under Pontius Pilate

crucifixus, mortuus, et sepultus,
kroo-chee-FEEK-soos MOHR-too-oos ayt say-POOL-toos
crucified dead and buried

4

descendit ad inferos,
day-SHAYN-deet ahd EEN-fay-ros
he-went-down to dead-ones

tertia die resurrexit a mortuis,
TAYRT-see-ah DEE-ay ray-soor-RAYK-seet ah MOHR-too-ees
on-third day he-rose from dead-ones

ascendit ad cælos, sedet ad dexteram
ah-SHAYN-deet ahd CHAY-lohs SAY-dayt ad DAYKS-tay-rahm
he-went-up to heavens he-sits at right-hand

Dei Patris omnipotentis, inde venturus
DAY-ee PAHT-rees ohm-nee-poh-TAYN-tis EEN-day vayn-TOO-roos
of-God of-FATHER of-Almighty from-there going-to-come

est iudicare vivos et mortuos.
ayst yoo-dee-KAH-ray VEE-vohs ayt MOHR-too-ohs
he-is to-judge living and dead

Credo in Spiritum Sanctum,
KRAY-doh een SPEE-ree-toom SAHNK-toom
I-believe in Spirit Holy

sanctam Ecclesiam catholicam,
SAHNK-tahm ayk-KLay-see-ahm ka-TOH-lee-kahm
holy Church universal

sanctorum communionem,
sahnk-TOH-room kohm-moo-nee-OH-naym
of-saints communion

remissionem peccatorum,
ray-mees-see-OH-naym payk-kah-TOH-room
remission of-sins

carnis resurrectionem,
KAHR-nees ray-soor-raykt-see-OH-naym
of-flesh resurrection

vitam æternam. Amen.
VEE-tahm ay-TAYR-noom AH-mayn
live eternal Amen

Our Father

Our Father, who art in heaven, hallowed be thy name. Thy kingdom come, thy will be done on earth as it is in heaven. Give us this day our daily bread, and forgive us our trespasses as we forgive those who trespass against us. And lead us not into temptation, but deliver us from evil. Amen.

Pater Noster qui es in cælis,
PAH-tayr NOHS-tayr kwee ays een CHAY-lees
Father Ours who are in heavens

Sanctificetur nomen tuum,
sahnk-tee-fee-CHAY-toor NOH-mayn TOO-oom
may-it-be-made-holy name yours

adveniat regnum tuum, fiat
ahd-VAY-nee-aht RAYN-yoom TOO-oom FEE-aht
may-it-come kingdom yours may-it-be-done

voluntas tua, sicut in cælo, et in terra.
voh-LOON-tahs TOO-ah SEE-koot een CHAY-loh ayt een TAY-ra
will yours as in heaven also in earth

Panem nostrum cotidianum da nobis
PAH-naym NOHS-troom koh-tee-dee-AH-noom dah NO-bees
Bread ours daily give to-us

hodie; et dimitte nobis debita nostra
HOH-dee-ay ayt dim-MITT-tay NOH-bees DAYH-bee-tah NOHS-tra
today; and take-away from-us debts ours

sicut et nos dimittimus debitoribus nostris;
See-koot ayt nohs dim-MITT-tim-moos daybit-TOHR-i-boos NOHS-trees
as also we we-take-away from-debts ours

et ne nos inducas in tentationem,
ayt nay nohs een-DOO-kahs een tayn-tahnt-see-OH-naym
and not us lead in temptation

sed libera nos a malo. Amen.
sayd LEE-bayar-ah nohs ah MAH-loh AH-mayn
but free us from evil Amen

Gloria Patri

Glory be to the Father, and to the Son, and to the Holy Spirit, as it was in the beginning, in now and ever shall be, world without end. Amen.

Gloria Patri et Filio et
GLOH-ree-ah PAH-tree ayt FEE-lee-oh ayt
Glory to-Father and to-Son and

Spiritui Sancto
spi-REE-too-ee SAHNK-toh
to-Spirit to-Holy

sicut erat in principio, et nunc et semper,
SEE-koot AY-raht een prin-CHEE-pee-oh ayt noonk ayt SAYM-payr
as it-was in beginning both now and always

in sæcula sæculorum. Amen.
een SAY-koo-lah say-koo-LOH-room AH-mayn
in ages of-ages Amen

Requiem Æternam

Eternal rest grant unto him/her (them), O Lord, and let perpetual light shine upon him/her (them). May he/she (they) rest in peace. Amen.

Requiem æternam dona ei (ea, eis), Domine,
RAY-kwee-aym ay-TAYR-nahm DOH-nah AY-ee (AY-ah AY-ees) DOH-mee-nay
Rest eternal give to-him (to-her, to-them) Lord

et lux perpetua luceat ei (ea, eis).
ayt looks payr-PAY-too-ah LOO-chay-aht AY-ee (AY-ah AY-ees)
and light everlasting may-it-shine on-him (on-her, on-them)

Requiescat (Requiescant) in pace. Amen.
ray-kwee-AY-schat (ray-kwee-AY-skahnt) een PAH-chay AH-mayn
may-he/she-rest (may-they-rest) in peace Amen

Salve, Regina

Hail holy Queen, Mother of mercy, our life, our sweetness and our hope. To thee do we cry poor banished children of Eve, To thee do we send up our sighs, mourning and weeping in this valley of tears. Turn then, most gracious advocate, thine eyes of mercy toward us. And after this, our exile, show us the blessed fruit of thy womb, Jesus. O clement, O loving, O sweet Virgin Mary.
Pray for us, O Holy Mother of God.
That we might be made worthy of the promises of Christ

Salve, Regina, mater misericordiæ, vita,
Sahl-vay ray-JEE-nah MAH-tayr mee-say-ree-KOHR-dee-ay VEE-tah
Hail Queen mother of-mercy life

dulcedo, et spes nostra, salve.
dool-CHAY-do ayt spays NOHS-trah SAHL-vay
sweetness and hope ours hail

Ad te clamamus, exsules filii
ahd tay klah-MAH-moos ayk-SOO-lays FEE-lee-yee
to-you we-cry-out banished children

Hevæ. Ad te suspiramus, gementes et flentes
HAY-vay ahd tay soos-pee-RAH-moos jay-MAYN-tays ayt FLAYN-tays
of-Eve towards you we-sigh groaning and weeping

in hac lacrimarum valle. Eia, ergo,
een hahk lah-kree-MAH-room VAHL-lay AY-yah AYR-goh
in this of-tears valley quick therefore

advocata nostra,
ahd-voh-KAH-tah NOHS-trah
advocate ours

illos tuos misericordes oculos
EEL-lohs TOO-ohs mee-say-ree-KOHR-days OH-koo-lohs
those your merciful eyes

ad nos converte.
ahd nohs kohn-VAYR-tay
towards us turn

Et Iesum, benedictum fructum ventris tui,
ayt YAY-soom bay-nay-DEEK-toom FROOK-toom VAYN-trees TOO-ee
and Jesus blessed fruit of-womb of-yours

nobis post hoc exsilium ostende.
NOH-bees post hohk ayks-SEE-lee-oom ohs-TAYN-day
to-us after this exile show

O clemens, O pia,
OH KLAY-mayns OH PEE-ah
O clement O loving

O dulcis Virgo Maria. Amen.
OH DOOL-chees VEER-goh mah-REE-ah AH-mayn
O sweet Virgin Mary Amen

V. Ora pro nobis, sancta Dei Genetrix.
OH-rah proh NOH-bees SAHNK-tah DAY-ee JAY-nee-treeks
Pray for us holy of-God Mother

R. Ut digni efficiamur
oot DEEN-yee ay-fee-chee-AH-moor
That worthy we-might-be-made

promissionibus Christi.
proh-mee-see-OH-nee-boos KREE-stee
for-promises of-Christ

B. Other Rosary Prayers

The Fatima Prayer

O my Jesus, forgive us our sins. Save us from the fires of hell. Lead all souls to heaven, especially those in most need of Thy mercy.

O Mi Iesu, dimitte nobis debita nostra
OH Mee YAY-soo dim-IT-tay NOH-bees DAYB-ee-tah NOHS-trah
O my Jesus release from-us debts ours

libera nos ab igne inferni
LEE-bayar-ah nohs ahb EEN-yay een-FAYR-nee
free us from fire of-hell

conduc in cælum omnes animas
KOHN-dook een CHAY-loom OHM-nays AH-nee-mas
lead into heaven all souls

præsertim illas quæ
pray-SAYR-tim EEL-lahs quay
especially those which

maxime indigent misericordia tua.
MAHK-see-may een-DEE-jaynt mee-say-ree-KOHR-dee-ah too-ah
to-the-greatest-extent they-need mercy yours

Final Prayer after the Salve Regina

Let us pray. O God, whose only-begotten Son, by his life, death, and resurrection, has purchased for use the rewards of eternal life, grant, we beseech Thee, that meditating upon these mysteries of the Most Holy Rosary of the Blessed Virgin Mary, we may imitate what they contain and obtain what they promise, through the same Christ our Lord. Amen.

Oremus: Deus, cuius Unigenitus
oh-RAY-moos DAY-oos KOO-yoos oo-ni-JAY-nee-toos
Let-us pray: God whose only-begotten-son

per vitam, mortem et resurrectionem suam
payr VEE-tahm MOHR-taym ayt ray-soo-raykt-see-OH-naym SOO-ahm
by life death and resurrection his

nobis salutis æternæ
NOH-bee sah-LOO-tees ay-TAYR-nay
to-us of-salvation of-eternal

præmia comparavit, concede, quæsumus:
pray-MEE-ah kohm-pah-RAH-veet kohn-CHAY-day KWAY-soo-moos
rewards has-bought grant we-pray

ut hæc mysteria sacratissimo beatæ
oot hayk mis-TAY-ree-ah sahk-rah-TEES-see-moh bay-AH-tay
that these mysteries from-most-holy of-blessed

Mariæ Virginis Rosario recolentes,
mah-REE-ay VEER-jee-nees roh-SAH-ree-oh ray-koh-LAYN-tays
of-Mary of-Virgin from-Rosary those-who-are-reflecting-upon

et imitemur quod continent,
ayt ee-mee-TAY-moor kwohd KOHN-tee-naynt
both we-might-imitate what they-contain

et quod promittunt assequamur.
ayt kwohd proh-MIT-toont ahs-say-KWAH-moor
and what they-promise we-might-obtain

Per eundem Christum Dominum nostrum. Amen.
payr ay-OON-daym KREES-toom DOH-mee-num NOHS-troom
Through same Christ Lord Ours Amen

C.   Prayers from the Ordinary of the Office

God, come to my assistance. Lord, make haste to help me.

Deus, in adiutorium meum intende.
Day-oos een ah-dee-yoo-TOH-ree-oom MAY-oom een-TAYN-day
God to assistance my come

Domine, ad adiuvandum meum festina.
DOH-mee-nay ahd ah-dee-yoo-VAHN-doom MAY-oom fays-TEE-nah
Lord to helping my hurry

Gloria Patri

Glory be to the Father, and to the Son, and to the Holy Spirit, as it was in the beginning, is now and ever shall be, world without end. Amen. Alleluia

Gloria Patri et Filio et
GLOH-ree-uh PAH-tree ayt FEE-lee-oh et
Glory to-Father and to-Son and

Spiritui Sancto
spi-REE-too-ee SAHNK-toh
to-Spirit to-Holy

sicut erat in principio, et nunc et semper,
SEE-koot AY-raht een prin-CHEE-pee-oh ayt noonk ayt SAYM-payr
as it-was in beginning both now and always

in sæcula sæculorum. Amen. Alleluia.
een SAY-koo-lah say-koo-LOH-room AH-mayn al-lay-LOO-yah
in ages of-ages Amen Praise-the-Lord

(in the office, the alleluia is only said after the Gloria after *Domine, ad adiuvandum*, and is omitted during Lent).

Benedictus

Blessed be the Lord, the God of Israel; he has come to his people and set them free. He has raised up for us a mighty savior, born of the house of his servant David. Through his holy prophets he promised of old, that he would save us from our enemies, from the hands of all who hate us. He promised to show mercy to our fathers and to remember his holy covenant. This was the oath he swore to our father Abraham, to set us free from the hands of our enemies, Free to worship him without fear, holy and righteous in his sight all the days of our life. You, my child, shall be called the prophet of the Most High, for you will go before the Lord to prepare his way, To give his people knowledge of salvation by the forgiveness of their sins. In the tender compassion of our God the dawn from on high shall break upon us, to shine on those who dwell in darkness and the shadow of death, and to guide our feet into the way of peace.

Benedictus Dominus Deus Israel,
bay-nay-DEEK-toos DOH-mee-noos DAY-oos AYSS-rah-ayl
Blessed (be) Lord God (of) Israel

quia visitavit, et fecit redemptionem
KWEE-ah vee-see-TAH-veet ayt FAY-cheet ray-daympt-see-OH-naym
for he-has-visited and he-made redemption

plebis suæ:
PLAY-bees SOO-AY
for-people for-his

Et erexit cornu salutis nobis
ayt ay-RAYK-sit KOHR-noo sah-LOO-tees NOH-bees
and he-raised-up horn of-salvation for-us

in domo David pueri sui.
een DOH-moh DAH-veed poo-AY-ree SOO-ee
in house (of) David of-son of-his

Sicut locutus est per os sanctorum,
SEE-koot loh-KOO-toos ayst payr os sahnk-TOH-room
as having-spoken he-is by mouth of-saints

qui a sæculo sunt, prophetarum eius:
kwee ah SAY-koo-loh soont proh-fay-TAH-room AY-yoos
who from ages are prophets his;

13

Salutem ex inimicis nostris,
Sah-LOO-taym ayks ee-nee-MEE-chees NOHS-trees
Deliverance out-of enemies ours

et de manu omnium qui oderunt nos:
ayt day MAH-noo OHM-nee-oom kwee OH-day-roont NOHS
and from hand of-all who hate us

Ad faciendam misericordiam
ahd fah-chee-AYN-dahm mee-say-ree-KOHR-dee-ahm
To performing mercy

cum patribus nostris:
koom PAH-tree-boos NOHS-trees
with forefathers ours

et memorari testamenti sui sancti:
ayt may-moh-RAH-ree tays-tah-MAYN-tee SOO-ee SANK-tee
and to-be-rememebred covenant his-own holy

Iusiurandum, quod iuravit ad Abraham
yoo-syoo-RAHN-doom kwohd yoo-RAH-veet ad AHB-rah-hahm
oath which he-swore to Abraham

patrem nostrum, daturum se nobis;
PAH-traym NOHS-troom dah-TOO-room say NOH-bees
father ours about-to-give himself to-us

Ut sine timore, de manu inimicorum
oot SEE-nay tee-MOH-ray day MAH-noo ee-nee-mee-KOH-room
that without fear from hand of-enemies

nostrorum liberati, serviamus illi.
nohs-TROH-room lee-bay-RAH-tee sayr-vee-AH-moos EEL-lee
ours free we-might-serve him

In sanctitate et iustitia coram ipso,
een sahnk-tee-TAH-tay ayt yoos-TEET-see-ah KOH-rahm EEP-soh
in holiness and justice before him

omnibus diebus nostris.
OHM-nee-boos dee-AY-boos NOHS-trees
through-all days ours

Et tu puer, propheta Altissimi vocaberis:
ayt TOO POO-ayr proh-FAY-tah ahl-TEES-see-mee voh-KAH-bay-rees
and you boy prophet of-the-Most-High you-shall-bee-called

14

præibis enim ante faciem Domini
pray-EE-bees AY-neem AHN-tay FAH-chee-aym DOH-mee-nee
you-shall-go for before face of-Lord

parare vias eius: Ad dandam
pah-RAH-ray VEE-ahs AY-yoosahd DAHN-dahm
to-prepare ways his: to giving

scientiam salutis plebi eius:
shee-AYNT-see-ahm sah-LOO-tees PLAY-bee AY-yoos
knowledge of-salvation to-people his

in remissionem peccatorum eorum:
een ray-mees-see-OH-naym payk-kah-TOH-room ay-OH-room
for remission of-sins theirs:

Per viscera misericordiæ Dei nostri:
payr VEE-shay-rah mee-say-ree-KOHR-dee-ay DAY-ee NOHS-tree
through heart mercies of-God ours:

in quibus visitabit nos, oriens ex alto:
een KWEE-boos vee-see-TAH-beet nohs OH-ree-ayns ayks AHL-to
in which he-shall-visit us calling from high

Illuminare his qui in tenebris
eel-loo-mee-NAH-ray hees kwee een tay-NAY-brees
to-illumine this which in darkness

et in umbra mortis sedent: ad dirigendos
ayt een OOM-brah MOHR-tees SAY-dayntahd dee-ree-JAYN-dohs
and in shadow of-death they-sit to guiding

pedes nostros in viam pacis.
PAY-days NOHS-trohs een VEE-ahm PAH-chees
feet ours in way of-peace

Magnificat

*My soul proclaims the greatness of the Lord, my spirit rejoices in
God my Savior; for he has looked with favor on his lowly servant.
From this day all generations will call me blessed: the Almighty has
done great things for me, and holy is his Name. He has mercy on
those who fear him in every generation. He has shown the strength
of his arm, he has scattered the proud in their conceit. He has cast
down the mighty from their thrones, and has lifted up the lowly. He
has filled the hungry with good things, and the rich he has sent away
empty. He has come to the help of his servant Israel, for he has
remembered his promise of mercy, The promise he made to our
fathers, to Abraham and his children for ever.*

Magnificat anima mea Dominum,
man-YEE-fee-kaht AH-nee-mah MAY-ah DOH-mee-noom
Magnifies soul mine Lord

et exultavit spiritus meus
ayt ayk-sool-TAH-veet SPEE-ree-toos MAY-oos
and exalts spirit mine

in Deo salvatore meo, quia respexit
een DAY-oh sahl-vah-TOH-ray may-oh KWEE-ah rays-PAYK-seet
in God savior mine because he-has-looked-at

humilitatem ancillæ suæ.
hoo-mee-lee-TAH-taym ahn-CHEEL-lay SOO-ay
humility of-handmaid of-his

Ecce enim ex hoc beatam me dicent
ACH-cha AY-neem ayks hohl bay-AH-tahm may DEE-chaynt
behold for out-of this blessed me shall-call

omnes generationes,
OHM-nays jay-nay-raht-see-OH-nays
all generations

quia fecit mihi magna, qui potens est,
KWEE-ah FAY-cheet MEE-hee MAHN-yah kwee POH-tayns ayst
because he-has-done to-me great-things who powerful is

et sanctum nomen eius,
ayt SAHNK-tahm NOH-mayn AY-yoos
and holy name his

16

et misericordia eius in progenies
ayt mee-say-ree-KOHR-dee-ah AY-yoos een proh-JAY-nee-ays
and mercy his in progeny

et progenies timentibus eum.
ayt proh-JAY-nee-ays tee-MAY-tee-boos AY-oom
and progeny to-those-who-fear him

Fecit potentiam in brachio suo,
FAY-cheet poh-TAYNT-see-ahm een BRAH-kee-oh SOO-oh
he-has-made powerful in arm his

dispersit superbos mente cordi sui;
dees-PAYR-seet soo-PAYR-bohs MAYN-tay KOHR-dee SOO-ee
he-has-scattered proud-ones   in-mind of-heart of-theirs

deposuit potentes de sede
day-POH-soo-eet poh-TAYN-tays day SAY-day
he-has-thrown-down powerful-ones from seat

et exaltavit humiles;
ayt ayk-sahl-TAH-veet HOO-mee-lays
and he-has-exalted humble-ones

esurientes implevit bonis
ay-soo-ree-AYN-tays eem-PLAY-veet
hungry-ones he-has-filled with-good-things

et divites dimisit inanes.
ayt dee-VEE-tays dee-MEE-seet ee-NAH-nays
and rich-ones he-has-sent-away empty

Suscepit Israel puerum suum,
soo-SHAY-peet EES-rah-ayl POO-ay-room SOO-oom
he-has-received Israel son his

recordatus misericordiæ,
ray-kohr-DAH-toos mee-say-ree-KOHR-dee-ay
having-called-to-mind mercy

sicut locutus est ad patres nostros,
SEE-koot loh-KOO-toos ayst ahd PAH-trays NOHS-trohs
as having-spoken he-is to fathers ours

Abraham et semini eius in sæcula.
AH-brah-ham ayt SAY-mee-nee AY-yoos een SAY-koo-lah
Abraham and seed his unto ages

Nunc Dimittis

Lord, you now have set your servant free to go in peace as you have promised; For these eyes of mine have seen the Savior, whom you have prepared for all the world to see: A Light to enlighten the nations, and the glory of your people Israel.

Nunc dimittis servum tuum, Domine
noonk di-MEET-tis SAYR-voom TOO-oom DOH-mee-nay
now you-dismiss servant yours Lord

Secundum verbum tuum in pace:
say-KOON-doom VAYR-boom TOO-oom in PAH-chay
according-to word yours in peace

Quia viderunt oculi mei
KWEE-ah vee-DAY-roont OH-koo-lee MAY-ee
because have-seen eyes mine

salutare tuum. Quod parasti ante
sah-loo-TAH-ray TOO-oom kwohd pah-RAHS-tee AHN-tay
salvation yours which you-have-prepared before

faciem omnium populorum:
FAH-chee-aym OHM-nee-oom poh-poo-LOH-room
face of-all of-people

Lumen ad revelationem gentium,
LOO-mayn ahd ray-vay-laht-see-OH-naym JAYNT-see-oom
light to revelation of-people

Et gloriam plebis tuæ Israel.
ayt GLOH-ree-am PLAY-bees TOO-ay EES-rah-ayl
and glory of-people of-yours Israel

D.   The Mass

Opening Rite of the Mass
In the name of the Father and of the Son and of the Holy Spirit
Amen

P. In nomine Patris, et Filii,
Een NOH-mee-nay PAH-trees ayt FEE-lee-yee
in name of-Father and of-Son

et Spiritus Sancti
ayt SPEE-ree-toos SAHNK-tee
and of-Spirit of-Holy
R. Amen

1. First Salutation Option

P. The grace of our Lord Jesus Christ, and the Love of God, and the fellowship of the Holy Spirit be with you all.

R. And also with you

P. Gratia Domini nostri Iesu Christi,
GRAHT-see-ah DOH-mee-nee NOHS-tree YAY-soo KREES-tee
grace of-Lord of-ours of-Jesus of-Christ

et caritas Dei, et communicatio
ayt KAH-ree-tahs DAY-ee ayt kohm-moo-nee-KAHT-see-oh
and love of-God and fellowship

Sancti Spiritus sit cum omnibus vobis.
SAHNK-tee SPEE-ree-toos sit koom OHM-nee-boos VOH-bees
of-Holy of-Spirit may-it-be with all you

R. Et cum spiritu tuo.
ayt koom SPEE-ree-too TOO-oh
and with spirit yours

2. Second Salutation Option

The grace and peace of God the Father and the Lord Jesus Christ be with you.

And Also with you

P. Gratia vobis et pax a Deo
GRAHT-see-ah VOH-bees ayt PAHKS AH DAY-oh
grace to-you and peace from God

Patre nostro et Domino Iesu Christo.
PAH-tray NOHS-troh ayt DOH-mee-noh YAY-soo KREES-toh
Father ours and Lord Jesus Christ

R. Benedictus Deus et Pater Domini
bay-nay-DEEK-toos DAY-oos ayt PAH-tayr DOH-mee-nee
Blessed God and Father of-Lord

nostri Iesu Christi.
NOHS-tree JAY-soo KREES-tee
of-ours of-Jesus of-Christ

3. Third Salutation Option

The Lord be with you.

And also with you.

P. Dominus Vobiscum
DOH-mee-nos voh-BEES-koom
Lord with-you

R. Et cum spiritu tuo.
et koom SPEE-ree-too TOO-oh
and with spirit yours

Confiteor - Pre-Vatican II

I confess to almighty God, to blessed Mary ever Virgin, to blessed Michæl the Archangel, to blessed John the Baptist, to the holy apostles Peter and Paul, and to all the saints that I have sinned exceedingly in thought, word, and deed, through my fault, through my fault, through my most grievous fault. Therefore, I beseech blessed Mary ever Virgin, blessed Michæl the Archangel, blessed John the Baptist, the holy apostles Peter and Paul, and all the saints, to pray for me to the Lord our God. Amen.

Confiteor Deo omnipotenti,
kohn-FEE-tay-ohr DAY-oh ohm-nee-poh-TAYN-tee
I-confess to-God alimighty

beatæ Mariæ semper Virgini,
bay-AH-tay mah-REE-ay SAYM-payr VEER-jee-nee
to-blessed to-Mary always to-Virgin

beato Michæli Archangelo,
bay-AH-toh mee-KAY-lee ahrk-AHN-jay-loh
to-blessed to-Michæl to-Archangel

beato Ioanni Baptistæ,
bay-AH-toh yoh-AHN-nee bahp-TEES-tay
to-blessed to-John to-Baptist

sanctis Apostolis Petro et Paulo,
SAHNK-tees ah-pohs-TOH-lees PAY-troh ayt POW-loh
to-holy-ones to-Apostles to-Peter and to-Paul

et omnibus Sanctis,
ayt OMH-nee-boos SAHNK-tees
and to-all to-Saints

quia peccavi nimis cogitatione,
KWEE-ah payk-KAH-vee NEE-mees koh-jee-taht-see-OH-nay
that I-have-sinned exceedingly by-thought

verbo et opere: mea culpa, mea culpa,
VAYR-boh ayt OH-pay-ray MAY-ah KOOL-pah MAY-ah KOOL-pah
by-word and by-work: by-my by-fault by-my by-fault

mea maxima culpa.
MAY-ah MAH-see-mah KOOL-pah
by-my by-most-grievous by-fault

22

Ideo precor beatam Mariam
EE-day-oh PRAY-kohr bay-AH-tahm mah-REE-ahm
Therefore I-ask blessed Mary

semper Virginem,
SAYM-payr VEER-jee-naym
always Virgin

beatum Michælem Archangelum,
bay-AH-toom mee-KAY-laym ahrk-AHN-jay-loom
blessed Michæl Archangel

beatum Ioannem Baptistam,
bay-AH-toom yo-AHN-naym bahp-TEES-tahm
blessed John Baptist

sanctos Apostolos Petrum et Paulum,
SAHNK-tohs ah-poh-STOH-lohs PAY-troom ayt POW-loom
holy Apostles Peter and Paul

et omnes Sanctos,
ayt OHM-nays SAHNK-tohs
and all Saints

orare pro me ad Dominum Deum nostrum. Amen.
oh-RAH-ray proh may ahd DOH-mee-noom DAY-oom NOHS-troom
to-pray for me to Lord God ours Amen

Confiteor - Post-Vatican II

I confess to almighty God, and to you, my brothers and sisters, that I have sinned through my own fault in my thoughts and in my words, in what I have done, and in what I have failed to do; and I ask blessed Mary, ever virgin, all the angels and saints, and you, my brothers and sisters, to pray for me to the Lord our God. Amen.

Confiteor Deo omnipotenti,
kohn-FEE-tay-ohr DAY-oh ohm-nee-poh-TAYN-tee
I-confess to-God almighty

et vobis, fratres, quia peccavi
ayt VOHS FRAH-traysKWEE-ah payk-KAH-vee
and to-you brothers that I-have-sinned

 nimis cogitatione, verbo, opere,
 NEE-mees koh-jee-taht-see-OH-nay VAYR-boh OH-pay-ray
exceedingly by-thought by-word by-work

et omisione: mea culpa, mea culpa,
ayt oh-mee-see-OH-nay MAY-ah KOOL-pah MAY-ah KOOL-pah
and by-omission: by-my by-fault by-my by-fault

mea maxima culpa.
MAY-ah MAH-see-mah KOOL-pah
by-my by-most-grievous by-fault

Ideo precor beatam Mariam
EE-day-oh PRAY-kohr bay-AH-tahm mah-REE-ahm
Therefore I-ask blessed Mary

semper Virginem,
SAYM-payr VEER-jee-naym
always Virgin

omnes Angelos et Sanctos, et vos, fratres,
OHM-nays AHN-jay-lohs ayt SAHNK-tohs ayt vohs FRAHT-rays
all angels and Saints and you brothers

orare pro me ad Dominum Deum nostrum. Amen.
oh-RAH-ray proh may ahd DOH-mee-noom DAY-oom NOHS-troom
to-pray for me to Lord God ours Amen

Kyrie

Lord have mercy. Christ have mercy. Lord have mercy.

Kyrie eleison.
KEE-ree-ay ay-LAY-ee-sohn
Lord have-mercy

Christe eleison.
KREES-tay ay-LAY-ee-sohn
Christ have-mercy

Kyrie eleison.
KEE-ree-ay ay-LAY-ee-sohn
Lord have-mercy

The Kyrie is the only portion of the Mass which retains the original language of the Church, Greek.

Gloria in Excelsis

Gloria in excelsis Deo, et in terra
GLOH-ree-ah een ayksCHAYL-sees DAY-oh ayt een TAYR-rah
Glory in high-places to-God and in earth

pax hominibus bonæ voluntatis.
pahks hoh-MEE-nee-boos BOH-nay voh-loon-TAH-tees
peace to-humans of-good of-will

Laudamus te, benedicimus te,
low-DAH-moos tay bay-nay-DEE-chee-moos tay
we-praise you we-bless you

adoramus te, glorificamus te, gratias
ah-doh-RAH-moos tay gloh-ree-fee-KAH-moos tay GRAHT-see-ahs
we-adore you we-glorify you thanks

agimus tibi propter magnam gloriam tuam,
AH-jee-moos TEE-bee PROHP-tayr MAHN-yam GLO-ree-am TOO-am
we-give to-you because-of great glory yours

Domine Deus, Rex cælestis,
DOH-mee-nay DAY-oos rayks chay-LAYS-tees
LORD GOD King heavenly

Deus Pater omnipotens.
DAY-oos PAH-tayr ohm-NEE-poh-tayns
GOD Father almighty

Domine Fili unigenite, Iesu Christe,
DOH-mee-nay FEE-lee oo-nee-JAY-nee-tay YAY-soo KREES-tay
Lord Son only-begotten Jesus Christ

Domine Deus, Agnus Dei,
DOH-mee-nay DAY-oos AHN-yoos DAY-ee
Lord God Lamb of-God

Filius Patris, qui tollis peccata
FEE-lee-oos PAHT-rees kwee TOHL-lees payk-KAH-tah
Son of-Father who takes-away sins

mundi miserere nobis;
MOON-dee mee-say-RAY-ray NOH-bees
of-world be-merciful to-us;

qui tollis peccata mundi,
kwee TOHL-lees payk-KAH-tah MOON-dee
who takes-away sins of-world

suscipe deprecationem nostram.
SOO-shee-pay day-pray-kaht-see-OH-naym NOHS-tram
receive prayer ours

Qui sedes ad dexteram Patris, miserere nobis.
kwee SAY-days ahd DAYKS-tay-ram PAHT-rees mee-say-RAY-ray NOH-bees
Who sits at right-hand of-Father be-merciful to-us

Domine Fili unigenite, Iesu Christe, Domine Deus,
DOH-mee-nay FEE-lee oo-nee-JAY-nee-tay YAY-soo KREES-tay DOH-mee-nay DAY-oos
Lord Son only-begotten Jesus Christ Lord God

Agnus Dei, Filius Patris,
AHN-yoos DAY-ee FEE-lee-oos PAHT-rees
Lamb of-God Son of-Father

qui tollis peccata mundi,
kwee TOHL-lees payk-KAH-tah MOON-dee
Who takes-away sins of-world

miserere nobis;
mee-say-RAY-ray NOH-bees
be-merciful to-us

qui tollis peccata mundi,
kwee TOHL-lees payk-KAH-tah MOON-dee
who takes-away sins of-world

suscipe deprecationem nostram.
SOO-shee-pay day-pray-kaht-see-OH-naym NOHS-tram
receive prayer ours

Qui sedes ad dexteram Patris,
kwee SAY-days ahd DAYKS-tay-rahm PAHT-rees
Who sits at right-hand of-Father

miserere nobis;
mee-say-RAY-ray NOH-bees
be-merciful to-us

Quoniam tu solus Sanctus, tu solus Dominus,
KWOH-nee-ahm too SOH-loos SAHNK-toos too SOH-loos DOH-mee-noos
because you only Holy you only Lord

tu solus Altissimus, Iesu Christe,
too SOH-loos ahl-TEE-see-moos YAY-soo KREES-tay
you only Highest Jesus Christ

cum Sancto Spiritu in gloria Dei Patris. Amen.
koom SAHNK-toh SPEE-ree-too een GLOH-ree-ah DAY-ee PAHT-rees
with Holy Spirit in glory of-God of-Father Amen

At the Readings

After the Old Testament and Epistle

The Word of the Lord. Thanks be to God

P. Verbum Domini
VAYR-boom DOH-mee-nee
Word of-Lord

R. Deo gratias.
DAY-oh GRAHT-see-ahs
to-God thanks

Before the Gospel

A reading from the holy Gospel according to . . .

P. Lectio sancti Evangelii secundum . . .
LAYKT-see-oh SAHNK-tee ay-vahn-JAY-lee-yee say-KOON-doom
Reading of-holy of-Gospel according-to

R. Gloria tibi, Domine.
GLOH-ree-ah TEE-bee DOH-mee-nee
Glory to-you Lord

After the Gospel

The Word of the Lord. Praise to you Lord Jesus Christ

P. Verbum Domini
VAYR-boom DOH-mee-nee
Word of-Lord

R. Laus tibi, Christe.
LOWs TEE-bee KREES-tay
Praise to-you Christ

Nicene Creed

I believe in one God, the Father almighty, maker of heaven and earth, and of all things visible and invisible. And in one Lord, Jesus Christ, the only begotten Son of God, born of the Father before all ages. God from God, Light from Light, true God from true God, begotten, not made, one in being with the Father; through Whom all things were made. Who for us men and for our salvation came down from heaven. He was made flesh by the Holy Spirit from the Virgin Mary, and was made man. He was crucified for us under Pontius Pilate; suffered, and was buried. On the third day He rose again according to the Scriptures; He ascended into heaven and sits at the right hand of the Father. He will come again in glory to judge the living and the dead, and of His kingdom there shall be no end. And in the Holy Spirit, the Lord and giver of Life, Who proceeds from the Father and the Son. Who, with the Father and the Son, is adored and glorified: Who has spoken through the Prophets. And I believe in one holy, catholic and apostolic Church. I confess one baptism for the remission of sins. And I look for the resurrection of the dead, and the life of the age to come. Amen.

Credo in unum Deum, Patrem omnipotentem,
KRAY-doh een OO-noom DAY-oom PAH-traym ohm-nee-poh-TAYN-taym
I-believe in one God Father Almighty

factorem cæli et terræ,
fahk-TOH-raym CHAY-lee ayt TAYR-ray
creator of-heave and of-earth

visibilium omnium et invisibilium.
vee-see-BEE-lee-oom OHM-nee-oom ayt een-vee-see-BEE-lee-oom
of-visible all and of-invisible

Et in unum Dominum Iesum Christum,
ayt een OO-noom DOH-mee-noom YAY-soom KREES-toom
and in one Lord Jesus Christ

Filium Dei unigenitum,
FEE-lee-oom DAY-ee oo-nee-JAY-nee-toom
Son of-God only-begotten

et ex Patre natum ante omnia sæcula.
ayt ayks PAH-tray NAH-toom AHN-tay OHM-nee-ah SAY-koo-lah
and from Father born before all ages

29

Deum de Deo, Lumen de Lumine,
DA-oom day DAY-oh LOO-mayn day LOO-mee-nay
God from God Light from Light

Deum verum de Deo vero,
DAY-oom VAY-room day DAY-oh VAY-roh
God true from God true

genitum non factum,
JAY-nee-toom nohn FAHK-toom
begotten not made

consubstantialem Patri;
kohn-soob-stahnt-see-AH-laym PAH-tree
of-the-same-substance with-Father;

per quem omnia facta sunt.
payr kwaym OHM-nee-ah FAHK-tah soont
through whom all-things having-been-made are

Qui propter nos homines
kwee PROHP-tayr nohs HOH-mee-nays
Who on-account-of us humans

et propter nostram salutem
ayt PROHP-tayr NOHS-trahm sah-LOO-taym
and on-account-of our salvation

descendit de cælis.
day-SHAYN-deet day CHAY-lees
he-has-come-down from heavens

Et incarnatus est de Spiritu Sancto
ayt een-kahr-NAH-toos ayst day SPEE-ree-too SAHNK-toh
and incarnate he-is by Holy Spirit

ex Maria Virgine, et homo factus est.
ayks mah-REE-ah VEER-jee-nay ayt HOH-moh FAHK-toos ayst
out-of Mary Virgin and human having-been-made is

Crucifixus etiam pro nobis
kroo-chee-FEEK-soos AYT-see-ahm proh NOH-bees

sub Pontio Pilato,
soob POHNT-see-oh pee-LAH-toh
under Pontius Pilate

passus et sepultus est,
PAHS-soos ayt say-POOL-toos ayst
having-suffered and having-been-buried he-is

et resurrexit tertia die,
ayt ray-soor-RAYK-seet TAYRT-see-ah DEE-ay
and he-rose-from-the-dead on-the-third day

secundum Scripturas,
say-KOON-doom skreep-TOO-rahs
according-to Scriptures

et ascendit in cælum,
ayt ah-SHAYN-deet een CHAY-loom
and ascended into heaven

sedet ad dexteram Patris.
SAY-dayt ahd DAYKS-tay-rahm PAH-trees
he-sits at right-hand of-Father

Et iterum venturus est cum gloria,
ayt EE-tay-room vayn-TOO-roos ayst koom GLOH-ree-ah
and again will-be-coming he-is with glory

iudicare vivos et mortuos,
yoo-dee-KAH-ray VEE-vohs ayt MOHR-too-ohs
to-judge living-ones and dead-ones

cuius regni non erit finis.
KOO-yoos RAYN-yee nohn AY-reet FEE-nees
whose reign not it-shall-be end

Et in Spiritum Sanctum,
ayt een SPEE-ree-toom SAHNK-toom
and in Spirit Holy

Dominum et vivificantem,
DOH-mee-noom ayt vee-vee-fee-KAHN-toom
Lord and life-giver

qui ex Patre Filioque procedit.
kwee ayks PAH-tray fee-lee-OH-kway
who from Father and-Son proceeds

Qui cum Patre et Filio simul adoratur
kwee koom PAH-tray ayt FEE-lee-oh SEE-mul ah-doh-RAH-toor
who with Father and Son together he-is-adored

31

et conglorificatur:
ayt kohn-glo-ree-fee-KAH-toor
and glorified-together

qui locutus est per prophetas.
kwee loh-KOO-toos ayst payr proh-FAY-tahs
who having-spoke is by prophets

Et unam, sanctam, catholicam
ayt OO-nahm SAHNK-tahm kah-TOH-lee-kahm
and one holy universal

et apostolicam Ecclesiam.
ayt ah-pohs-TOH-lee-kahm ay-KLAY-see-ahm
and apostolic Church

Confiteor unum baptisma
kohn-FEE-tay-ohr OO-noom bahp-TEES-mah
I-confess one baptism

in remissionem peccatorum.
een ray-mees-see-OH-naym payk-kah-TOH-room
for remission of-sins

Et expecto resurrectionem mortuorum,
ayt ayks-PAYK-toh ray-soor-raykt-see-OH-naym mohr-too-OH-room
and await resurrection of-dead-ones

et vitam venturi sæculi. Amen.
ayt VEE-tahm vayn-TOO-ree SAY-koo-lee AH-mayn
and life of-coming of-age Amen

At the Eucharistic Prayer, before the Preface

P. Pray, brethren, that our sacrifiece may be acceptable to God, the almighty Father.

R. May the Lord accept the sacrifice at your hands for the praise and glory of his name, for our good, and the good of all his Church.

P. Orate, fratres: ut meum ac vestrum
oh-RAH-tay FRAHT-rays oot MAY-oom ahk VAYS-troom
Pray brothers: thay my and your

sacrificium acceptabile fiat
sahk-ree-FEE-chee-oom ahk-chayp-TAH-bee-lay FEE-aht
sacrifice acceptible it-might-be-made

apud Deum Patrem omnipotenem.
AH-pood DAY-oom PAHT-raym ohm-nee-poh-TAYN-taym
in-the-presence-of God Father omnipotent

R. Suscipiat Dominus sacrificium
soo-SHEE-pee-aht DOH-mee-noos sahk-ree-FEE-chee-oom
may-he-receive Lord sacrifice

de manibus tuis ad laudem
day MAH-nee-boos TOO-ees ahd LOW-daym
from hands yours to praise

et gloriam nominis sui,
ayt GLOH-ree-ahm NOH-mee-nees SOO-ee
and glory of-name of-his

ad utilitatem quoque
ahd oo-tee-lee-TAH-taym KWOH-kway
to benefit also

nostram totiusque Ecclesiæ suæ sanctæ.
NOHS-trahm toht-see-OOS-kway ayk-KLAY-see-ay soo-ay SAHNK-tay
ours and-all of-church of-his of-holy

P. The Lord be with you.

R. And also with you.

P. Lift up your hearts

R. We lift them up to the Lord

P. Let us give thanks to the Lord our God.

R. It is right to give him thanks and praise.

P. Dominus vobiscum
DOH-mee-noos voh-BEES-koom
Lord with-you

R. Et cum spiritu tuo
ayt koom SPEE-ree-too TOO-oh
and with spirit yours

P. Sursum Corda
SOOR-soom KOHR-dah
upward hearts

R. Habemus ad Dominum.
hah-BAY-moos ad DOH-mee-noom
we-have to Lord

P. Gratias agamus Domino Deo nostro
GRAHT-see-ahs AH-gah-moos DOH-mee-noh DAY-oh NOHS-troh
thanks layt-us-givay to-Lord to-God to-ours

R. Dignum et iustum est.
DEEN-yoom ayt YOOS-toom ayst
Worthy and just it-is

At the Eucharistic Prayer, after the Preface

Holy, Holy, Holy, Lord God of Power and Might
Heaven and earth are full of your glory.
Hosanna in the highest.
Blessed is He who comes in the name of the Lord.
Hosanna in the highest.

Sanctus, sanctus, sanctus,
SAHNK-toos SAHNK-toos SAHNK-toos
Holy holy holy

Dominus Deus sabaoth.
DOH-mee-noos DAY-oos SAH-bah-oht
Lord God of-Hosts

Pleni sunt cæli et terra gloria tua.
PLAY-nee soont CHAY-lee ayt TAY-rah GLOH-ree-ah TOO-ah
Full are heavens and earth with-glory with-yours

Hosanna in excelsis.
hoh-SAHN-nah een ayks-CHAYL-sees
Hosanna in highest

Benedictus qui venit in nomine Domini.
bay-nay-DEEK-toos kwee VAY-neet een NOH-mee-nay DOH-mee-nee
Blessed who he-comes in name of-Lord

Hosanna in excelsis.
hoh-SAHN-nah een ayks-CHAYL-sees
Hosanna in highest

After the Consecration

P. Mysterium fidei.
mis-TAY-ree-oom fee-DAY-ee
Mystery of-faith

R. Mortem tuam annuntiamus Domine
MOHR-taym TOO-ahm ahn-noont-see-AH-moos DOH-mee-nay
Death yours we-announce Lord

et tuam resurrectionem confitemur,
ayt TOO-ahm ray-soor-raykt-see-OH-naym kohn-fee-TAY-moor
and yours resurrection we-confess

donec venias.
DOH-nayk VAY-nee-ahs
until you-shall-come

At the Peace

P. Pax Domini sit semper vobiscum.
pahks DOH-mee-nee seet SAYM-payr voh-BEES-koom
Peace of-Lord may-it be always with-you

R. Et cum spiritu tuo.
ayt koom SPEE-ree-too TOO-oh
and with spirit yours

Agnus Dei

Agnus Dei, qui tollis peccata mundi,
AHN-yoos DAY-ee kwee TOHL-lees payk-KAH-tah MOON-dee
Lamb of-God who you-take-away sins of-world

miserere nobis.
mee-say-RAY-ray NOH-bees
be-merciful to-us

Agnus Dei, qui tollis peccata mundi,
AHN-yoos DAY-ee kwee TOHL-lees payk-KAH-tah MOON-dee
Lamb of-God who you-take-away sins of-world

dona nobis pacem.
DOH-nah NOH-bees PAH-chaym
give to-us peace

At Communion

Priest:

Ecce Agnus Dei,
AY-chay AHN-yoos DAY-ee
behold Lamb of-God

ecce qui tollit peccava mundi.
AY-chay kwee TOHL-leet payk-KAH-vah MOON-dee
behold who takes-away sins of-world

Beati qui ad cenam Agni vocati sunt.
bay-AH-tee kwee ahd CHAY-nahm AHN-yee voh-KAH-tee soont
Blessed who to dinner of-Lamb called are

Priest and people:

Domine, non sum dignus,
DOH-mee-nay nohn soom DEEN-yoos
Lord not I-am worthy

ut intres sub tectum meum,
oot EEN-trays soob TAYK-toom MAY-oom
that you-enter under roof mine

sed tantum dic verbo
sayd TAHN-toom deek VAYR-boh
but just say word

et sanabitur anima mea.
ayt sah-NAH-bee-toor AHN-nee-mah May-ah
and it-will-be-healthy soul mine

The Dismissal

P. Ite, missa est.
EE-tay MEES-sah ayst
Go dismissed it-is

R. Deo gratias.
DAY-oh GRAHT-see-ahs
to-God thanks

E.   Benediction of the Blessed Sacrament

1. O Saving Victim opening wide
The gate of heaven to all below.
Our foes press on from every side;
Thine aid supply, Thy strength bestow.

2. To Thy great name be endless praise
Immortal Godhead, One in Three;
Oh, grant us endless length of days,
In our true native land with Thee.
Amen

1. O Salutaris Hostia
oh sah-loo-TAH-rees HOHS-tee-ah
O Saving Victim

Quæ cæli pandis ostium.
kway CHAY-lee PAHN-dees OHS-tee-oom
Which of-heaven you-open door

Bella premunt hostilia;
BAY-lah PRAY-moont hohs-TEE-lee-ah
wars they-oppose hostile-ones;

Da robur, fer auxilium.
dah ROH-boor fayr owk-SEE-lee-oom
give strength bring help

2. Uni trinoque Domino
OO-nee tree-NOH-kway DOH-mee-noh
to-one and-to-three to-Lord

Sit sempiterna gloria:
seet saym-pee-TAYR-nah GLOH-ree-ah
be everlasting glory;

Qui vitam sine termino,
kwee VEE-tahm SEE-nay TAYR-mee-noh
Who life without end

Nobis donet in patria. Amen.
NOH-hees DOH-nayt een PAH-tree-ah AH-mayn
to-us gives in home-land Amen

Tantum Ergo Sacramentum

1. Down in adoration falling,
Lo! the sacred Host we hail,
Lo! oe'r ancient forms departing
Newer rites of grace prevail;
Faith for all defects supplying,
Where the feeble senses fail.

1. Tantum ergo Sacramentum
TAHN-toom AYR-goh sah-krah-MAYN-toom
so-much therefore Sacrament

Veneremur cernui:
vay-nay-RAY-moor CHAYR-noo-ee
We-worship with-bowed-heads

Et antiquum documentum
ayt ahn-TEE-kwoom doh-koo-MAYN-toom
and ancient example

Novo cedat ritui:
NOH-voh CHAY-daht REE-too-ee
to-new gives-way to-rite:

Præstet fides supplementum
PRAYS-tayt FEE-days soop-lay-MAYN-toom
may-it-furnish faith supply

Sensuum defectui.
SAYN-soo-oom day-FAYK-too-ee
meaning to-sin

2. To the everlasting Father,
And the Son Who reigns on high
With the Holy Spirit proceeding
Forth from each eternally,
Be salvation, honor blessing,
Might and endless majesty.

2. Genitori, Genitoque
jay-nee-TOH-ree jay-nee-TOH-kway
To-Father and-to-Son

Laus et iubilatio,
lows ayt yoo-bee-LAHT-see-oh
Praise and gladness

Salus, honor, virtus quoque
SAH-loos HOH-nohr VEER-toos KWOH-kway
Salvation honor virtue also

Sit et benedictio:
seet ayt bay-nay-DEEKT-see-oh
May-it-be and blessing

Procedenti ab utroque
proh-chay-DAYN-tee ahb oo-TROHK-way
coming-forth from both-directions

Compar sit laudatio. Amen.
KOHM-pahr seet low-DAHT-see-oh AH-mayn
companion may-it-be praise Amen

V. You have given them bread from heaven,

R. Having all sweetness within it.

V. Panem de cælo præstitisti eis. (T. P. Alleluia)
PAH-naym day CHAY-loh pray-stee-TEES-tee AY-ees
Bread from heaven you-have-prescribed for-them

R. Omne delectamentum in se habentem. (T. P. Alleluia)
OHM-nay day-layk-tah-MAYN-toom een say hah-BAYN-taym
all source-of-delight in itself having

Let us pray:

O God, who in this wonderful Sacrament left us a memorial of Thy Passion: grant, we implore Thee, that we may so venerate the sacred mysteries of Thy Body and Blood, as always to be conscious of the fruit of Thy Redemption. Thou who livest and reignest forever and ever.

Oremus:
oh-RAY-moos
Let-us-pray

Deus, qui nobis sub sacramento mirabili,
DAY-oos kwee NOH-bees soob sahk-rah-MAYN-toh mee-RAH-bee-lee
God who to-us under sacrament marvelous

passionis tuæ memoriam reliquisti:
pahs-see-OH-nees TOO-ay may-MOH-ree-ahm ray-lee-KWEES-tee
of-passion of-yours memorial has-left:

tribue, quæsumus, ita nos corporis et
TREE-boo-ay KWAY-soo-moos EE-tah nohs kohr-POH-rees ayt
give we-pray thus we/us of-body and

sanguinis tui sacra mysteria venerari,
SAHN-gwee-nees TOO-ee SAH-krah mis-TAY-ree-ah vay-nay-RAH-ree
of-blood of-yours holy mystery to-venerate

ut redemptionis tuæ fructum
oot ray-daympt-see-OH-nees TOO-ay FROOK-toom
that of-redemption of-yours fruit

in nobis iugiter sentiamus.
een NOH-bees YOO-jee-tayr sayn-tee-AH-moos
in us continually we-might-experience

Qui vivis et regnas in sæcula sæculorum. Amen
kwee VEE-vees ayt RAYN-yahs een SAY-koo-lah say-koo-LOH-room
Who you-live and you-reign in ages of-ages Amen

Laudes Divinæ

Benedictus Deus.
bay-nay-DEEK-toos DAY-oos
Blessed (be) God

Benedictum Nomen Sanctum eius.
bay-nay-DEEK-toom NOH-mayn SAHNK-toom AY-yoos
Blessed (be) Name Holy his

Benedictus Iesus Christus,
bay-nay-DEEK-toos YAY-soos KREES-toos
Blessed (be) Jesus Christ

verus Deus et verus homo.
VAY-roos DAY-oos ayt VAY-roos HOH-moh
true God and true (hu)man

Benedictum Nomen Iesu.
bay-nay-DEEK-toom NOH-mayn YAY-soo
Blessed (be) Name of-Jesus

Benedictum Cor eius sacratissimum.
bay-nay-DEEK-toom KOHR AY-yoos sah-krah-TEE-see-moom
Blessed (be) Heart his most-holy

Benedictus Sanguis eius pretiosissimus.
bay-nay-DEEK-toos SAHN-gwees AY-yoos prayt-see-oh-SEE-see-moos
Blessed (be) Blood his most-precious

Benedictus Iesus in sanctissimo
bay-nay-DEEK-toos YAY-soos een sahnk-TEE-see-moh
Blessed (be) Jesus in most-holy

altaris Sacramento.
ahl-TAH-rees sah-krah-MAYN-toh
of-altar Sacrament

Benedictus Sanctus Spiritus, Paraclitus.
bay-nay-DEEK-toos SAHNK-toos SPEE-ree-toos pah-RAH-klee-toos
Blessed (be) Holy Spirit Paraclete

Benedicta excelsa Mater Dei,
bay-nay-DEEK-tah ayks-CHAYL-sah MAH-tayr DAY-ee
Blessed (be) glorious Mother of-God

Maria sanctissima.
mah-REE-ah sahnk-TEE-see-mah
Mary most-holy

Benedicta sancta eius et immaculata Conceptio.
bay-nay-DEEK-tah SAHNK-tah AY-yoos ayt eem-mah-koo-LAH-tah kohn-CHAYPT-see-oh
Blessed (be) holy hers and immaculate conception

Benedicta eius gloriosa Assumptio.
bay-nay-DEEK-tah AY-yoos gloh-ree-OH-sah ahs-SOOMPT-see-oh
Blessed (be) her glorious Assumption

Benedictum nomen Mariæ, Virginis et Matris.
bay-nay-DEEK-toom NOH-mayn mah-REE-ay VEER-jee-nees ayt MAH-trees
Blessed (be) name of-Mary Virgin and Mother

Benedictus sanctus Ioseph,
bay-nay-DEEK-toos SAHNK-toos YOH-sayf
Blessed (be) holy Joseph

eius castissimus Sponsus.
AY-yoos kahs-TEE-see-moos SPOHN-soos
her most-chaste Spouse

Benedictus Deus in Angelis suis,
bay-nay-DEEK-toos DAY-oos een AHN-jay-lees SOO-ees
Blessed (be) God in Angels his

et in Sanctis suis. Amen.
ayt een SAHNK-tees SOO-ees
and in Holy-ones his Amen

F.   Other prayers

O Lumen

Oh Light of the Church, Doctor of Truth
Rose of Patience, Ivory of Chastity,
You freely offered the Father of Wisdom;
Preacher of grace, unite us to the Blessed.
(Antiphon to St. Dominic)

O lumen Ecclesiæ
OH LOO-mayn ayk-KLAY-see-ay
O light of-Church

Doctor veritatis,
DOHK-tohr vay-ree-TAH-tees
Doctor of-truth

Rosa patientiæ,
ROH-sah paht-see-AYNT-see-ay
Rose of-patience

Ebur castitatis,
AY-boor kahs-tee-TAH-tees
Ivory of-chastity

Aquam sapientiæ
AH-kwahm sah-pee-AYNT-see-ay
Water of-wisdom

propinasti gratis,
proh-pee-NAHS-tee GRAH-tees
you-offered freely

Prædicator gratiæ,
pray-dee-KAH-tohr GRAHT-see-ay
preacher of-grace

nos junge beatis.
nohs YOON-gay bay-AH-tees
us join to-blessed-ones

Sancte Michæl Archangele

Saint Michæl the Archangel, defend us in battle. Be our protection against the wickedness and snares of the devil. May God rebuke him, we humbly pray; and do Thou, O Prince of the Heavenly Host by the Divine Power of God cast into hell, satan and all the evil spirits, who roam throughout the world seeking the ruin of souls. Amen.

Sancte Michæl Archangele,
SAHNK-tay MEE-kah-ayl ahrk-AHN-jay-lay
Holy Michæl Archangel

defende nos in proelio, contra nequitiam
day-FAYN-day nohs in PRAY-lee-oh KOHN-trah nay-KWEET-see-ahm
defend us in battle against wickedness

et insidias diaboli esto præsidium.
ayt een-SEE-dee-ahs dee-AH-boh-lee AYS-toh pray-SEE-dee-oom
and snares of-devil be protection

Imperet illi Deus, supplices deprecamur:
eem-PAY-rayt EEL-lee DAY-oos SOOP-plee-chays day-pray-KAH-moor
may-order him God (we)-humble-ones pray:

tuque, Princeps militiæ cælestis,
TOO-kway PREEN-chayps mee-LEET-see-ay chay-LAYS-tees
and-you Prince of-army of-celestial

Satanam aliosque spiritus malignos,
SAH-tah-nahm ah-lee-OHS-kway SPEE-ree-toos mah-LEEN-yohs
Satan and-other spirits evil

qui ad perditionem animarum
kwee ahd payr-deet-see-OH-naym ah-nee-MAH-room
who for ruin of-souls

pervagantur in mundo, divina virtute,
payr-vah-GAHN-toor een MOON-doh dee-VEE-nah veer-TOO-tay
wander-through in world by-divine by-power

in infernum detrude. Amen
een een-FAYR-noom day-TROO-day AH-mayn
into hell thrust-down Amen

The Angelus

V. Angelus Domini nuntiavit Mariæ;
AHN-jay-loos DOH-mee-nee noont-see-AH-veet mah-REE-ay
Angel of-Lord has-announced to-Mary

R. Et concepit de Spiritu Sancto.
ayt kohn-CHAY-peet day SPEE-ree-too SAHNK-toh
and she-conceived from Spirit Holy

V. Ecce ancilla Domini.
AYCH-chay ahn-CHEEL-lah DOH-mee-nee
behold handmaid of-Lord

R. Fiat mihi secundum verbum tuum.
FEE-aht MEE-hee say-KOON-doom VAYR-boom TOO-oom
may-it-be-done to-me according-to word yours

V. Et Verbum caro factum est.
ayt VAYR-boom KAH-roh FAHK-toom ayst
and Word flesh been-made has

R. Et habitavit in nobis.
ayt hah-bee-TAH-veet in NOH-bees
and he-dwelled among us

V. Ora pro nobis, sancta Dei Genetrix.
OH-rah proh NOH-bees SAHNK-tah DAY-ee JAY-nay-treeks
Pray for us holy of-God Mother

R. Ut digni efficiamur promissionibus Christi.
oot DEEN-yee ayf-fee-chee-AH-moor proh-mees-see-OH-nee-boos KREES-tee
That worthy we-might-be-made for-the-promises of-Christ

Oremus: Gratiam tuam, quæsumus,
oh-RAY-moos GRAHT-see-ahm TOO-ahm KWAY-soo-moos
let-us-pray grace yours we-pray

Domine, mentibus nostris infunde;
DOH-mee-nay MAYN-tee-boos NOHS-trees in-FOON-day
Lord souls ours pour-into;

ut qui, Angelo nuntiante,
oot kwee AHN-jay-loh noont-see-AHN-tay
that who by-angel announced

Christi Filii tui incarnationem
KREE-stee FEE-lee-ee TOO-ee een-kahr-naht-see-OH-naym
of-Christ of-Son of-yours incarnation

cognovimus, per passionem eius et crucem,
kohn-yoh-VEE-moos payr pahs-see-OH-naym AY-yoos ayt KROO-chaym
we-might-know by passion his and cross

ad resurrectionis gloriam perducamur.
ahd ray-soor-raykt-see-OH-nees GLO-ree-ahm payr-doo-KAH-moor
to of-resurrection glory we-might-be-led

Per eundem Christum Dominum nostrum.
payr ay-OON-daym KREES-toom DOH-mee-noom NOHS-troom
through same Christ Lord ours

R. Amen.
Amen

Regina Cæli, Lætare, Alleluia

Queen of Heaven, rejoice, alleluia:
for he whom you merited to bear, alleluia:
Has risen, as he said, alleluia:
Pray for us to God, alleluia.
V. *Rejoice and be glad, O Virgin Mary, alleluia.*
R. *Because the Lord is truly risen, alleluia.*

Regina cæli, lætare, alleluia:
ray-GEE-nah CHAY-lee lay-TAH-ray ah-lay-LOO-yah
queen of-heaven rejoice alleluia;

Quia quem meruisti portare, alleluia.
KWEE-ah kwaym may-roo-AYSS-tee pohr-TAH-ray ah-lay-LOO-yah
because he-who you-merited to-bear alleluia

Resurrexit sicut dixit, alleluia.
ray-soor-RAYK-seet SEE-koot DEEK-seet ah-lay-LOO-yah
he-has-risen-again as he-said ah-lay-LOO-yah

Ora pro nobis Deum, alleluia.
OH-rah proh NOH-bees DAY-oom ah-lay-LOO-yah
Pray for us to-God alleluia

V. Gaude et lætare, Virgo Maria, alleluia,
GAH-oo-day ayt lay-TAH-ray VEER-go mah-REE-ah ah-lay-LOO-yah
be-glad and rejoice Virgin Mary Alleluia

R. Quia surrexit Dominus vere, alleluia.
KWEE-ah soor-RAYK-seet DOH-mee-noos VAY-ray ah-lay-LOO-yah
because has-risen-again Lord truly alleluia

Confiteor - Pre-Vatican II

Confiteor Deo omnipotenti, beatæ Mariæ semper Virgini, beato Michæli Archangelo, beato Ioanni Baptistæ, sanctis Apostolis Petro et Paulo, et omnibus Sanctis, quia peccavi nimis cogitatione, verbo et opere: mea culpa, mea culpa, mea maxima culpa. Ideo precor beatam Mariam semper Virginem, beatum Michælem Archangelum, beatum Ioannem Baptistam, sanctos Apostolos Petrum et Paulum, et omnes Sanctos, orare pro me ad Dominum Deum nostrum. Amen.

Confiteor - Post-Vatican II

Confiteor Deo omnipotenti, et vobis, fratres, quia peccavi nimis cogitatione, verbo, opere, et omisione: mea culpa, mea culpa, mea maxima culpa. Ideo precor beatam Mariam semper Virginem, omnes Angelos et Sanctos, et vos, fratres, orare pro me ad Dominum Deum nostrum. Amen.

Kyrie

Kyrie eleison. Christe eleison. Kyrie eleison.

Gloria in Excelsis

Gloria in excelsis Deo, et in terra pax hominibus bonæ voluntatis. Laudamus te, benedicimus te, adoramus te, glorificamus te, gratias agimus tibi propter magnam gloriam tuam, Domine Deus, Rex cælestis, Deus Pater omnipotens. omine Fili unigenite, Iesu Christe, Domine Deus, Agnus Dei, Filius Patris, qui tollis peccata mundi miserere nobis; qui tollis peccata mundi, suscipe deprecationem nostram. Qui sedes ad dexteram Patris, miserere nobis. Domine Fili unigenite, Iesu Christe, Domine Deus, Agnus Dei, Filius Patris, qui tollis peccata mundi, miserere nobis; qui tollis peccata mundi, suscipe deprecationem nostram. Qui sedes ad dexteram Patris, miserere nobis; Quoniam tu solus Sanctus, tu solus Dominus, tu solus Altissimus, Iesu Christe, cum Sancto Spiritu in gloria Dei Patris. Amen.

At the Readings

After the Old Testament and Epistle

P. Verbum Domini

R. Deo gratias.

Before the Gospel

P. Lectio sancti Evangelii secundum . . .

R. Gloria tibi, Domine.

After the Gospel

P. Verbum Domini

R. Laus tibi, Christe.

Nicene Creed

Credo in unum Deum, Patrem omnipotentem, factorem cæli et terræ, visibilium omnium et invisibilium.

Et in unum Dominum Iesum Christum, Filium Dei unigenitum, et ex Patre natum ante omnia sæcula. Deum de Deo, Lumen de Lumine, Deum verum de Deo vero, genitum non factum, consubstantialem Patri; per quem omnia facta sunt. Qui propter nos homines et propter nostram salutem descendit de cælis. Et incarnatus est de Spiritu Sancto ex Maria Virgine, et homo factus est. Crucifixus etiam pro nobis sub Pontio Pilato, passus et sepultus est, et resurrexit tertia die, secundum Scripturas, et ascendit in cælum, sedet ad dexteram Patris. Et iterum venturus est cum gloria, iudicare vivos et mortuos, cuius regni non erit finis.

Et in Spiritum Sanctum, Dominum et vivificantem, qui ex Patre Filioque procedit. Qui cum Patre et Filio simul adoratur et conglorificatur: qui locutus est per prophetas. Et unam, sanctam, catholicam et apostolicam Ecclesiam. Confiteor unum baptisma in remissionem peccatorum. Et expecto resurrectionem mortuorum, et vitam venturi sæculi. Amen.

At the Eucharistic Prayer, before the Preface

P. Orate, fratres: ut meum ac vestrum sacrificium acceptabile fiat apud Deum Patrem omnipotenem.

R. Suscipiat Dominus sacrificium de manibus tuis ad laudem et gloriam nominis sui, ad utilitatem quoque nostram totiusque Ecclesiæ suæ sanctæ.

P. Dominus vobiscum

R. Et cum spiritu tuo

P. Sursum Corda

R. Habemus ad Dominum.

P. Gratias agamus Domino Deo nostro

R. Dignum et iustum est.

At the Eucharistic Prayer, after the Preface

Sanctus, sanctus, sanctus, Dominus Deus sabaoth. Pleni sunt cæli et terra gloria tua. Hosanna in excelsis. Benedictus qui venit in nomine Domini. Hosanna in excelsis.

After the Consecration

P. Mysterium fidei.

R. Mortem tuam annuntiamus Domine et tuam resurrectionem confitemur, donec venias.

At the Peace

P. Pax Domini sit semper vobiscum.

R. Et cum spiritu tuo.

Agnus Dei

Agnus Dei, qui tollis peccata mundi, miserere nobis.

Agnus Dei, qui tollis peccata mundi, miserere nobis.

Agnus Dei, qui tollis peccata mundi, dona nobis pacem.

At Communion

Priest:

Ecce Agnus Dei, ecce qui tollit peccava mundi. Beati qui ad cenam Agni vocati sunt.

Priest and people:

Domine, non sum dignus, ut intres sub tectum meum, sed tantum dic verbo et sanabitur anima mea.

The Dismissal

P. Ite, missa est.

R. Deo gratias.

E. Benediction of the Blessed Sacrament

O Salutaris

1. O Salutaris Hostia
Quæ cæli pandis ostium.
Bella premunt hostilia;
Da robur, fer auxilium.

2. Uni trinoque Domino
Sit sempiterna gloria:
Qui vitam sine termino,
Nobis donet in patria. Amen.

Tantum Ergo Sacramentum

1. Tantum ergo Sacramentum
Veneremur cernui:
Et antiquum documentum
Novo cedat ritui:
Præstet fides supplementum
Sensuum defectui.

2. Genitori, Genitoque
Laus et iubilatio,
Salus, honor, virtus quoque
Sit et benedictio:
Procedenti ab utroque
Compar sit laudatio. Amen.

V. Panem de cælo præstitisti eis. (T. P. Alleluia)

R. Omne delectamentum in se habentem. (T. P. Alleluia)

Oremus: *Deus, qui nobis sub sacramento mirabili, passionis tuæ memoriam reliquisti: tribue, quæsumus, ita nos corporis et sanguinis tui sacra mysteria venerari, ut redemptionis tuæ fructum in nobis iugiter sentiamus. Qui vivis et regnas in sæcula sæculorum. Amen*

Laudes Divinæ

Benedictus Deus.

Benedictum Nomen Sanctum eius.

Benedictus Iesus Christus, verus Deus et verus homo.

Benedictum Nomen Iesu.

Benedictum Cor eius sacratissimum.

Benedictus Sanguis eius pretiosissimus.

Benedictus Iesus in sanctissimo altaris Sacramento.

Benedictus Sanctus Spiritus, Paraclitus.

Benedicta excelsa Mater Dei, Maria sanctissima.

Benedicta sancta eius et immaculata Conceptio.

Benedicta eius gloriosa Assumptio.

Benedictum nomen Mariæ, Virginis et Matris.

Benedictus sanctus Ioseph, eius castissimus Sponsus.

Benedictus Deus in Angelis suis, et in Sanctis suis. Amen.

F.   Other prayers

O Lumen

O lumen Ecclesiæ
Doctor veritatis,
Rosa patientiæ,
Ebur castitatis,
Aquam sapientiæ
propinasti gratis,
Prædicator gratiæ,
nos junge beatis.

Sancte Michæl Archangele

Sancte Michæl Archangele, defende nos in proelio, contra nequitiam et insidias diaboli esto præsidium. Imperet illi Deus, supplices deprecamur: tuque, Princeps militiæ cælestis, Satanam aliosque spiritus malignos, qui ad perditionem animarum pervagantur in mundo, divina virtute, in infernum detrude. Amen

The Angelus

V. Angelus Domini nuntiavit Mariæ;

R. Et concepit de Spiritu Sancto.

Ave Maria . . .

V. Ecce ancilla Domini.

R. Fiat mihi secundum verbum tuum.

Ave Maria . . .

V. Et Verbum caro factum est.

R. Et habitavit in nobis.

Ave Maria . . .

V. Ora pro nobis, sancta Dei Genetrix.

R. Ut digni efficiamur promissionibus Christi.

Oremus: Gratiam tuam, quæsumus, Domine, mentibus nostris infunde; ut qui, Angelo nuntiante, Christi Filii tui incarnationem cognovimus, per passionem eius et crucem, ad resurrectionis gloriam perducamur. Per eundem Christum Dominum nostrum.
R. Amen.

Regina Cæli, Lætare, Alleluia

Regina cæli, lætare, alleluia:
Quia quem meruisti portare, alleluia.
Resurrexit sicut dixit, alleluia.
Ora pro nobis Deum, alleluia.

V. Gaude et lætare, Virgo Maria, alleluia,

R. Quia surrexit Dominus vere, alleluia.

Oremus:
Deus qui per resurrectionem Filii tui, Domini nostri Iesu Christi, mundum lætificare dignatus es: præsta, quæsumus, ut per eius Genetricem Virginem Mariam, perpetuæ capiamus gaudia vitæ. Per eundem Christum Dominum nostrum.

R. Amen.

Memorare

Memorare, O piissima Virgo Maria, non esse auditum a sæculo, quemquam ad tua currentem præsidia, tua implorantem auxilia, tua petentem suffragia, esse derelictum. Ego tali animatus confidentia, ad te, Virgo Virginum, Mater, curro, ad te venio, coram te gemens peccator assisto. Noli, Mater Verbi, verba mea despicere; sed audi propitia et exaudi Amen

Anima Christi

Anima Christi, sanctifica me.
Corpus Christi, salva me.
Sanguis Christi, inebria me.
Aqua lateris Christi, lava me.
Passio Christi, conforta me.
O bone Iesu, exaudi me.
Intra tua vulnera absconde me.
Ne permittas me separari a te.
Ab hoste maligno defende me.
In hora mortis meæ voca me.
Et iube me venire ad te,
Ut cum Sanctis tuis laudem te
in sæcula sæculorum. Amen.

Act of Contrition

Deus meus, ex toto corde pænitet me omnium meorum peccatorum, eaque detestor, quia peccando, non solum poenas a Te iuste statutas promeritus sum, sed præsertim quia offendi Te, summum bonum, ac dignum qui super omnia diligaris. Ideo firmiter propono, adiuvante gratia Tua, de cetero me non peccaturum peccandique occasiones proximas fugiturum. Amen.

Prayers of The Chaplet of Divine Mercy

Pater æterne, offero tibi Corpus et Sanguinem, animam et divinitatem dilectissimi Filii Tui, Domini nostri, Iesu Christi, in propitiatione pro peccatis nostris et totius mundi.

Pro dolorosa Eius passione, miserere nobis et totius mundi.

Sanctus Deus, Sanctus Fortis, Sanctus Immortalis, miserere nobis et totius mundi.

Ave Verum Corpus

Ave verum Corpus natum
De Maria Virgine:
Vere passum, immolatum
In cruce pro homine:

Cuius latus perforatum
Fluxit aqua et sanguine:
Esto nobis praegustatum
Mortis in examine.

O Iesu dulcis! O Iesu pie!

O Iesu Fili Mariae. Amen

G. Enchiridion of Indulgences — Pious Invocations

Adoramus te, Christe, et benedicimus tibi; quia per Crucem tuam redemisti mundum.

Benedicta sit sancta Trinitas.

Christus vincit! Christus regnat! Christus imperat!

Cor Iesu, flagrans amore nostri, inflamma cor nostrum amore tui.

Cor Iesu, in te confido.

Cor Iesu, omnia pro te.

Cor Iesu sacratissimum, miserere nobis.

Deus meus et omnia.

Deus, propitius esto mihi peccatori.

Dignare me laudare te, Virgo sacrata; da mihi virtutem contra hostes tuos.

Dominus meus et Deus meus!

Dulce cor Mariæ, esto salus mea.

Iesu, Maria, Ioseph.

Iesu, Maria, Ioseph, vobis cor et animam meam dono.

Iesu, Maria, Ioseph, adstate mihi in extremo agone.

Iesu, Maria, Ioseph, in pace vobiscum dormiam et requiescam.

Mane nobiscum, Domine.

Mater dolorosa, ora pro nobis.

Mater mea, fiducia mea.

O crux, ave, spes unica.

Omnes Sancti et Sanctæ Dei, orate pro nobis.

Pater, in manus tuas commendo spiritum meum.

Sancta Maria, Mater Dei, ora pro me.

Tu es Christus, Filius Dei vivi.

Notes

Made in the USA
Lexington, KY
08 June 2012